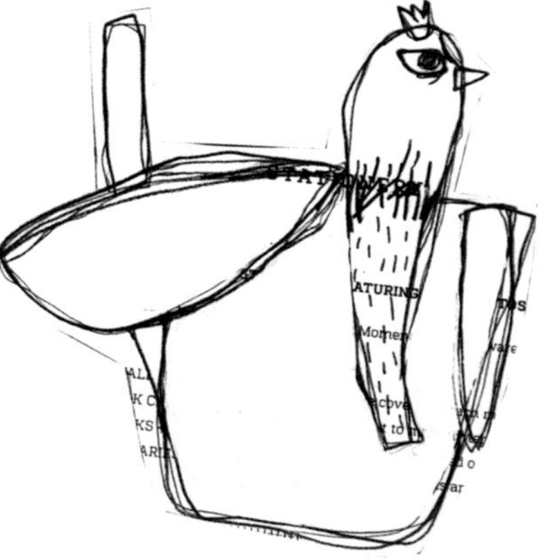

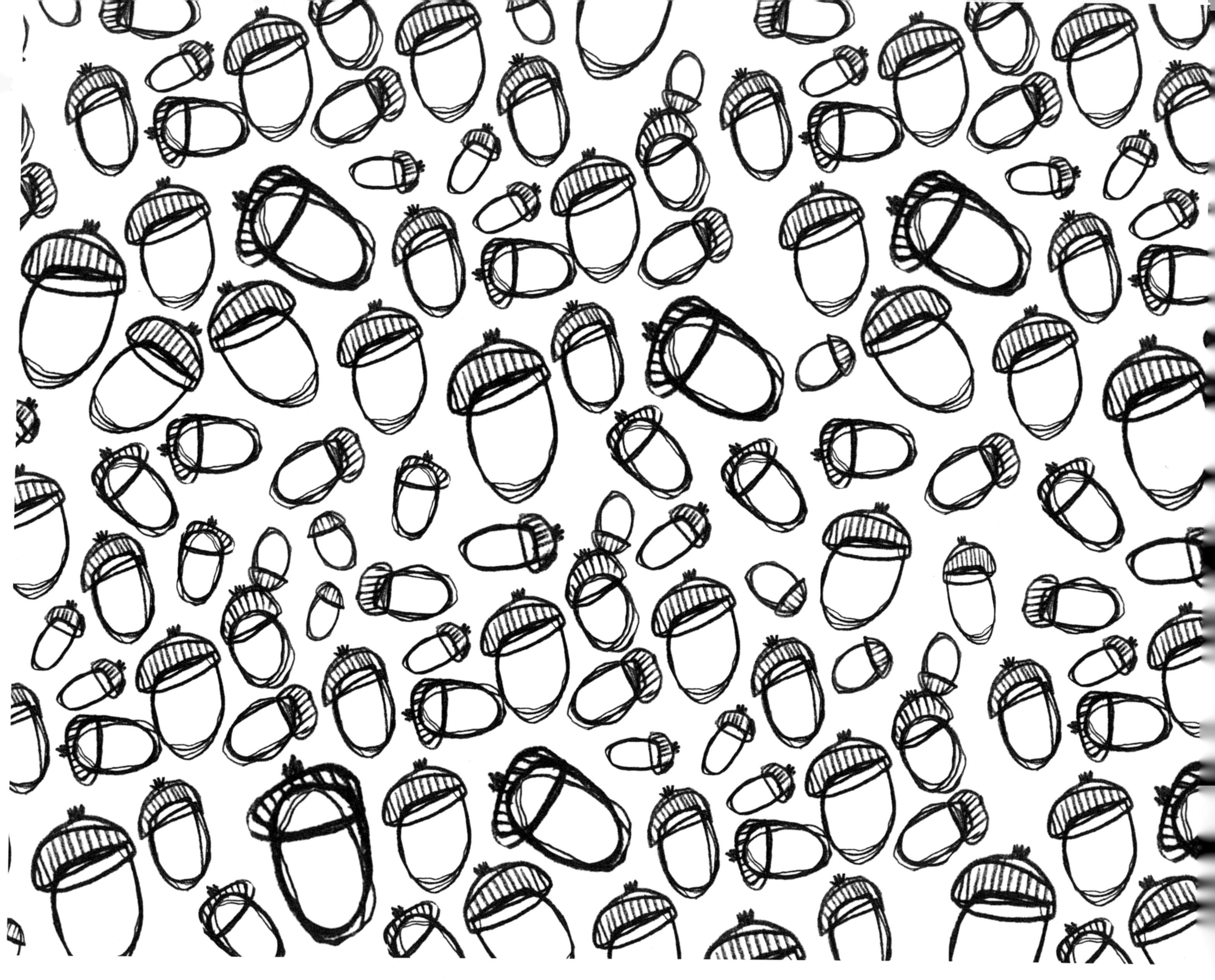

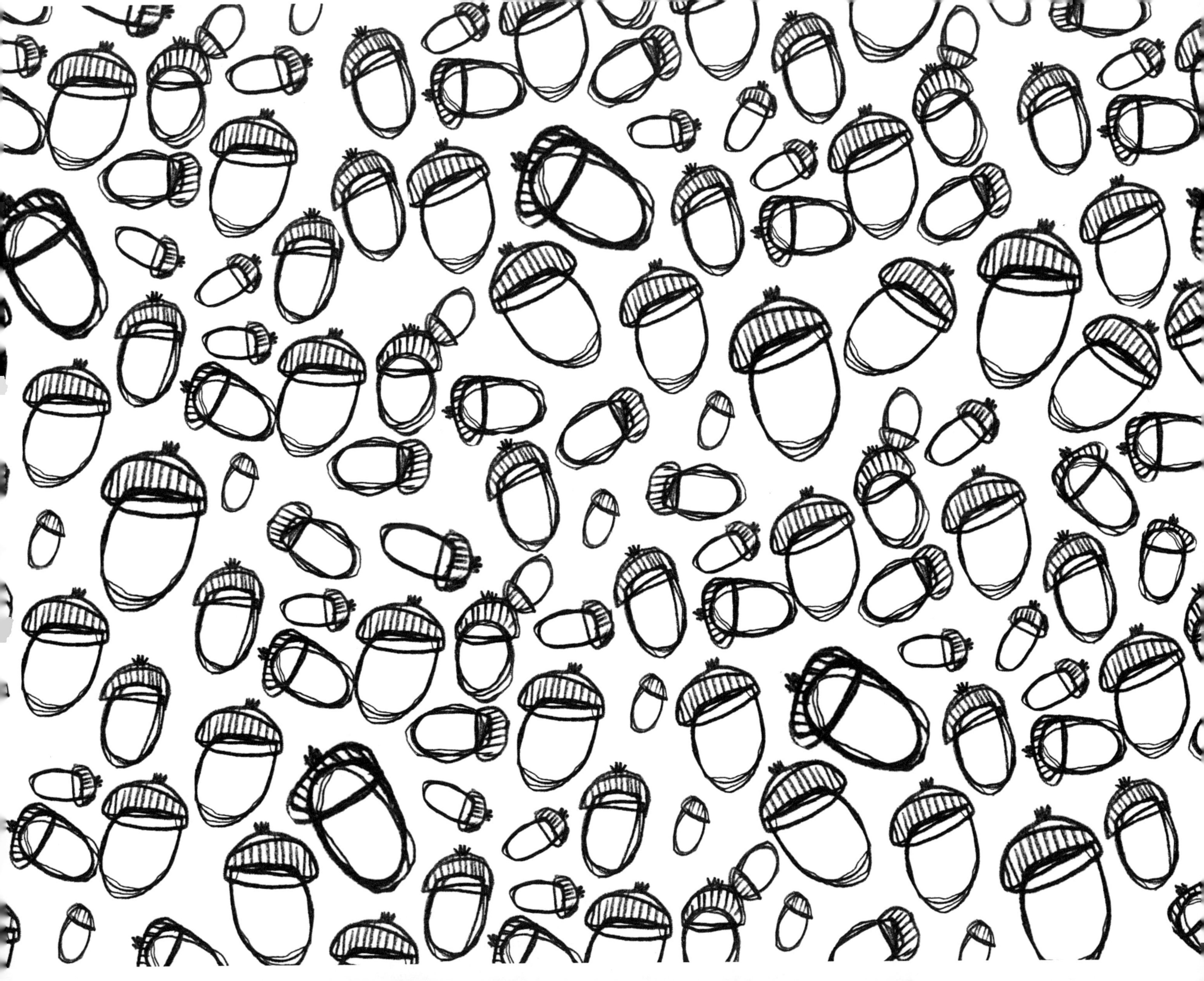

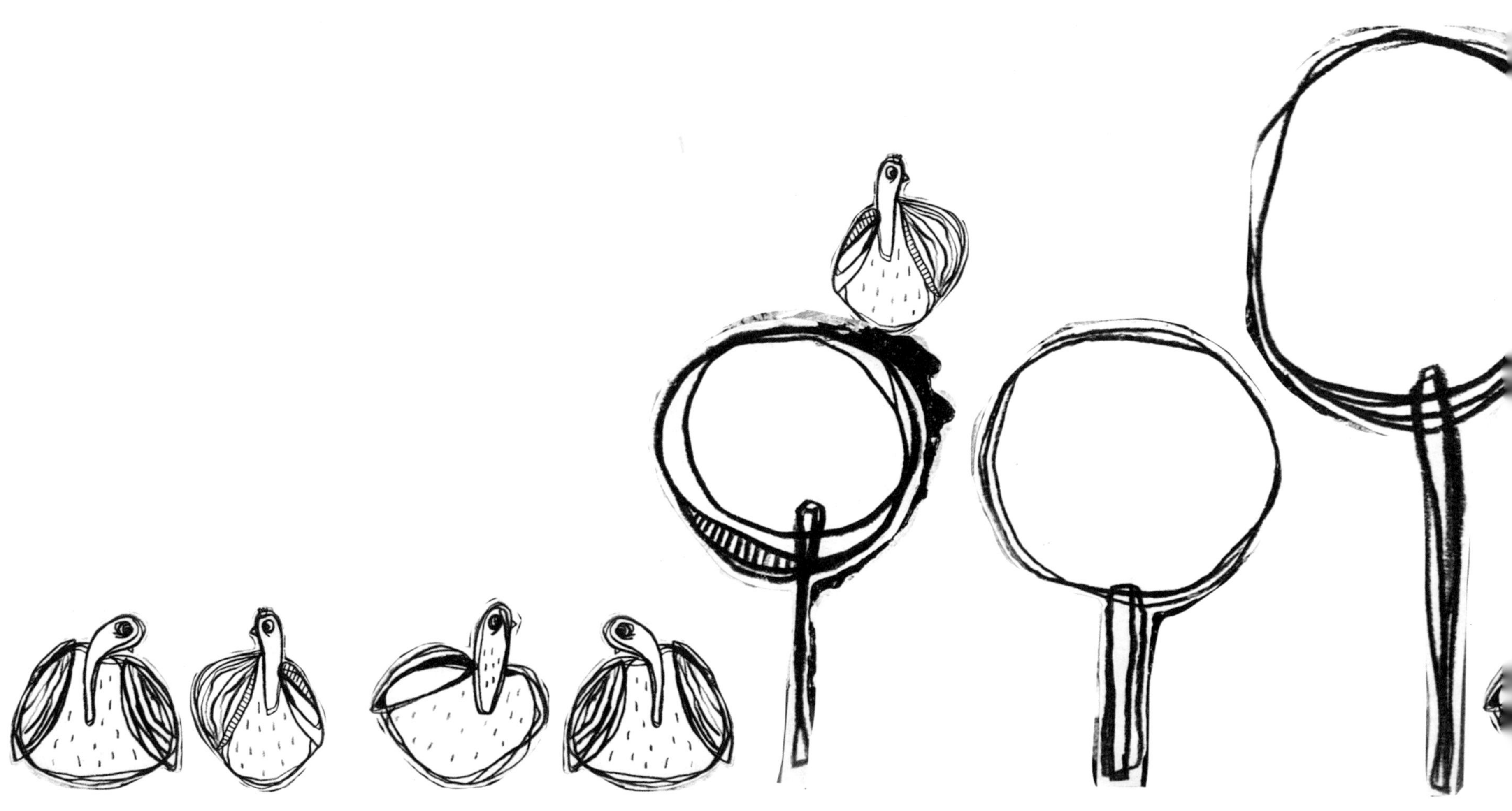

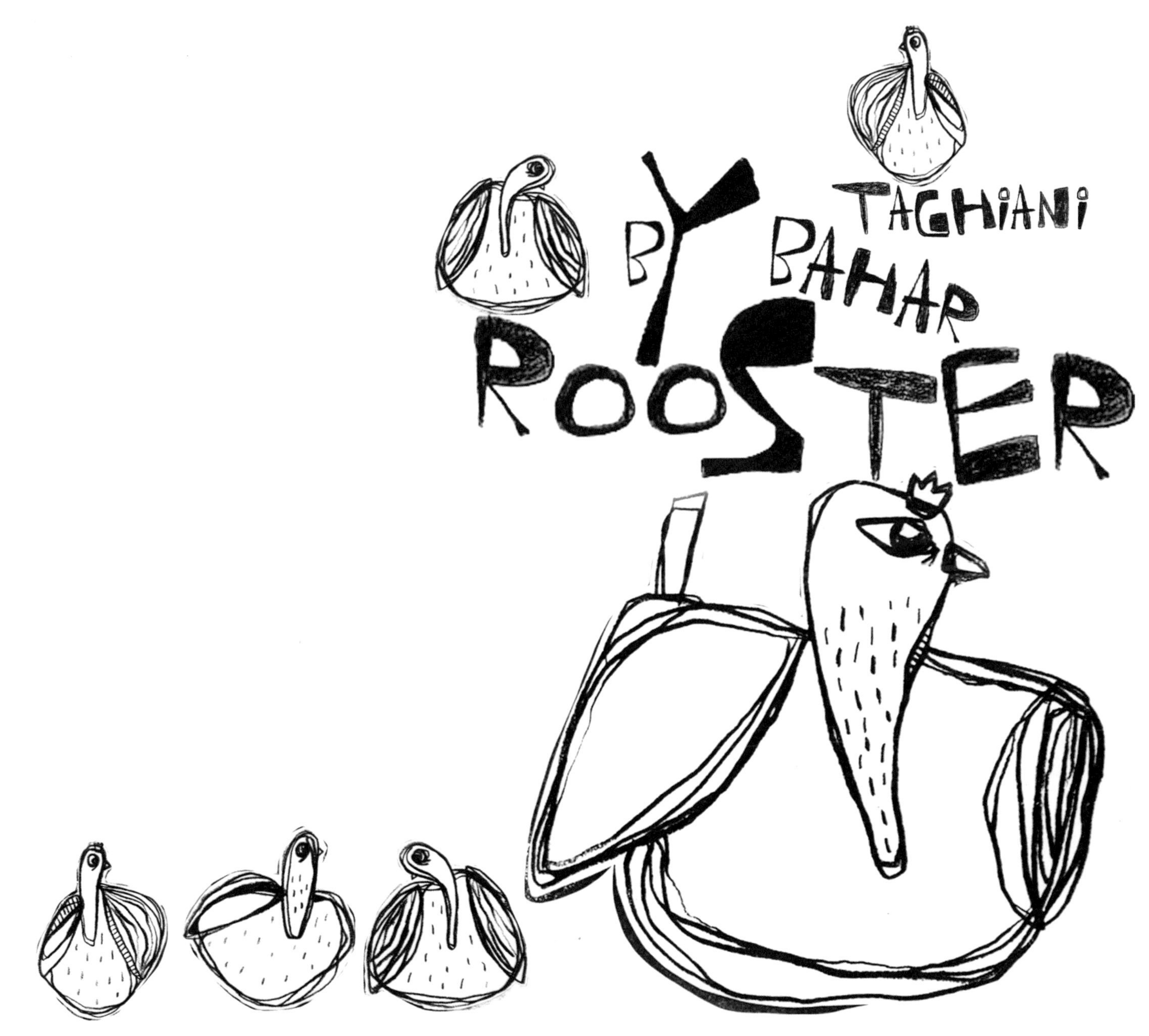

BY TAGHIANI BAHAR
ROOSTER

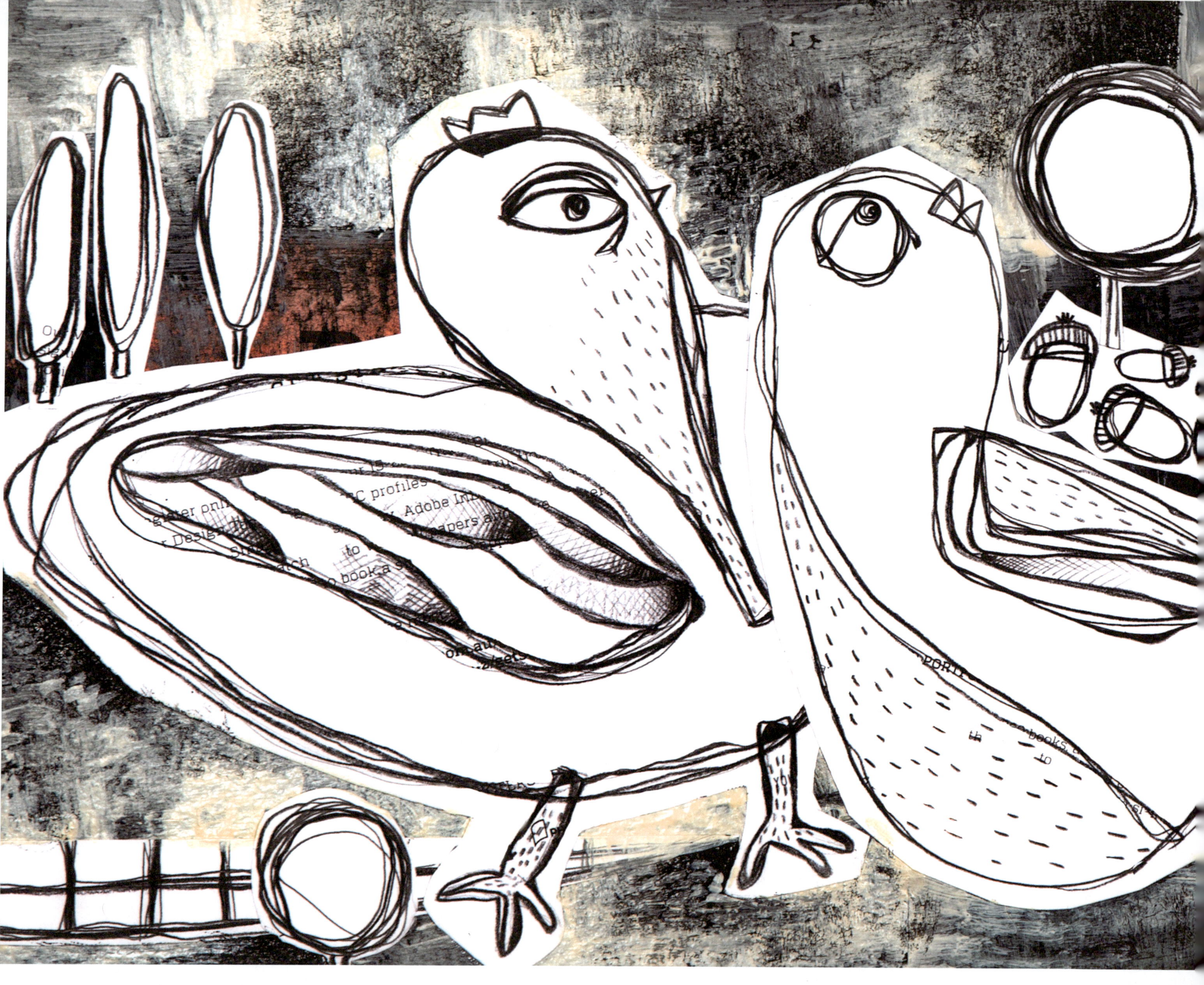

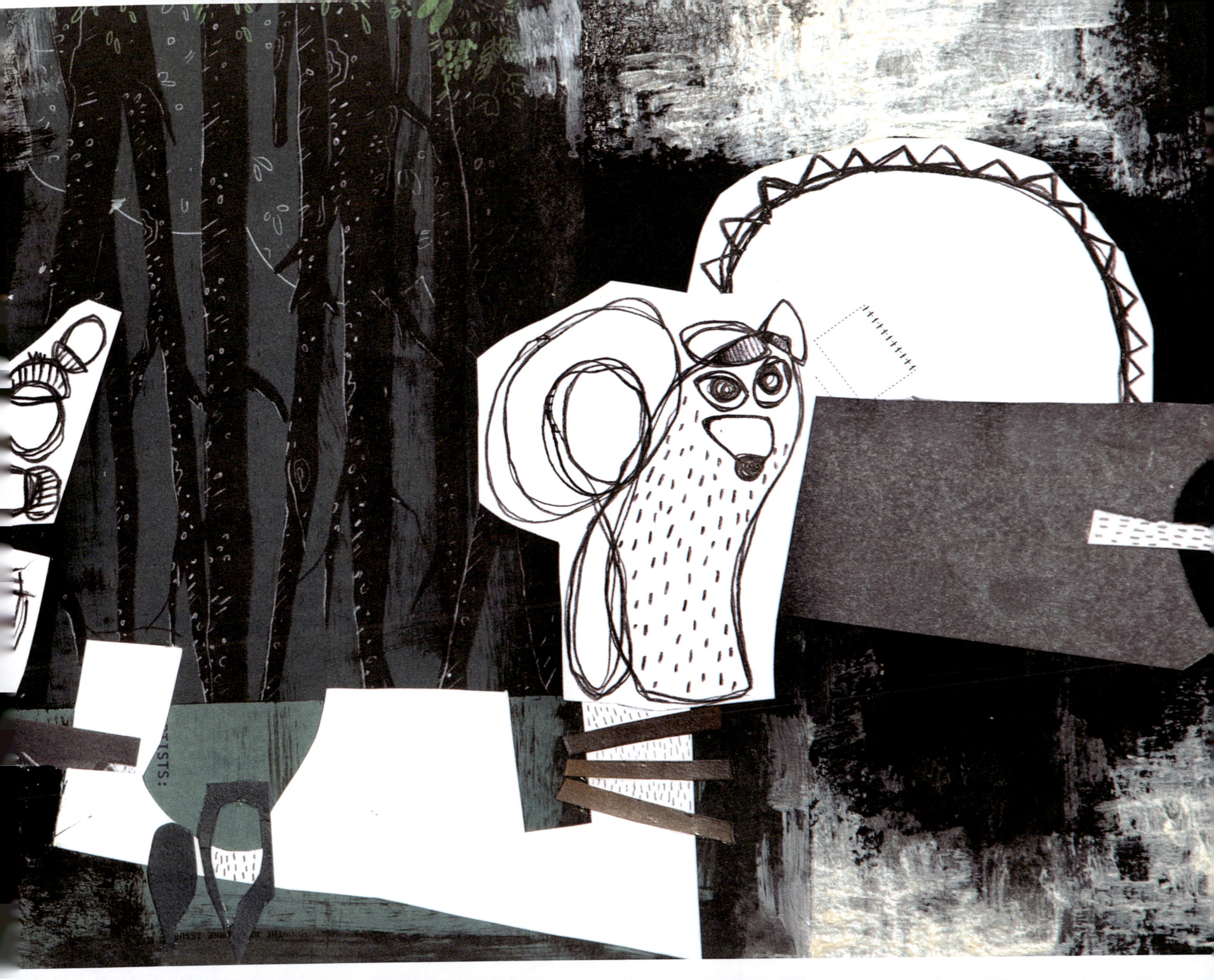

THE ROOSTER AND THE HEN HAVE OAK FRUITS.

A FOX IS BESIDE THE SUNRISE.

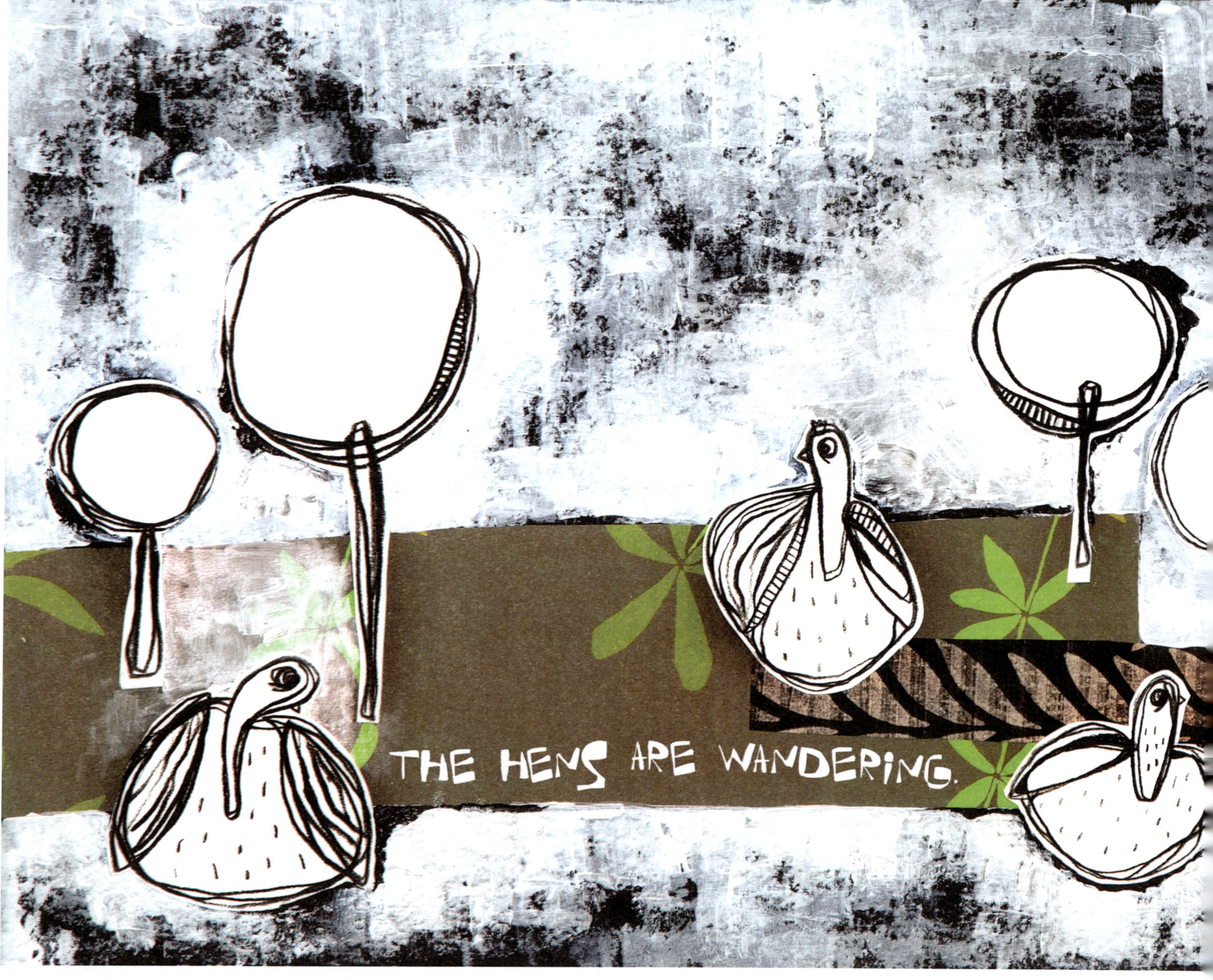
THE HENS ARE WANDERING.

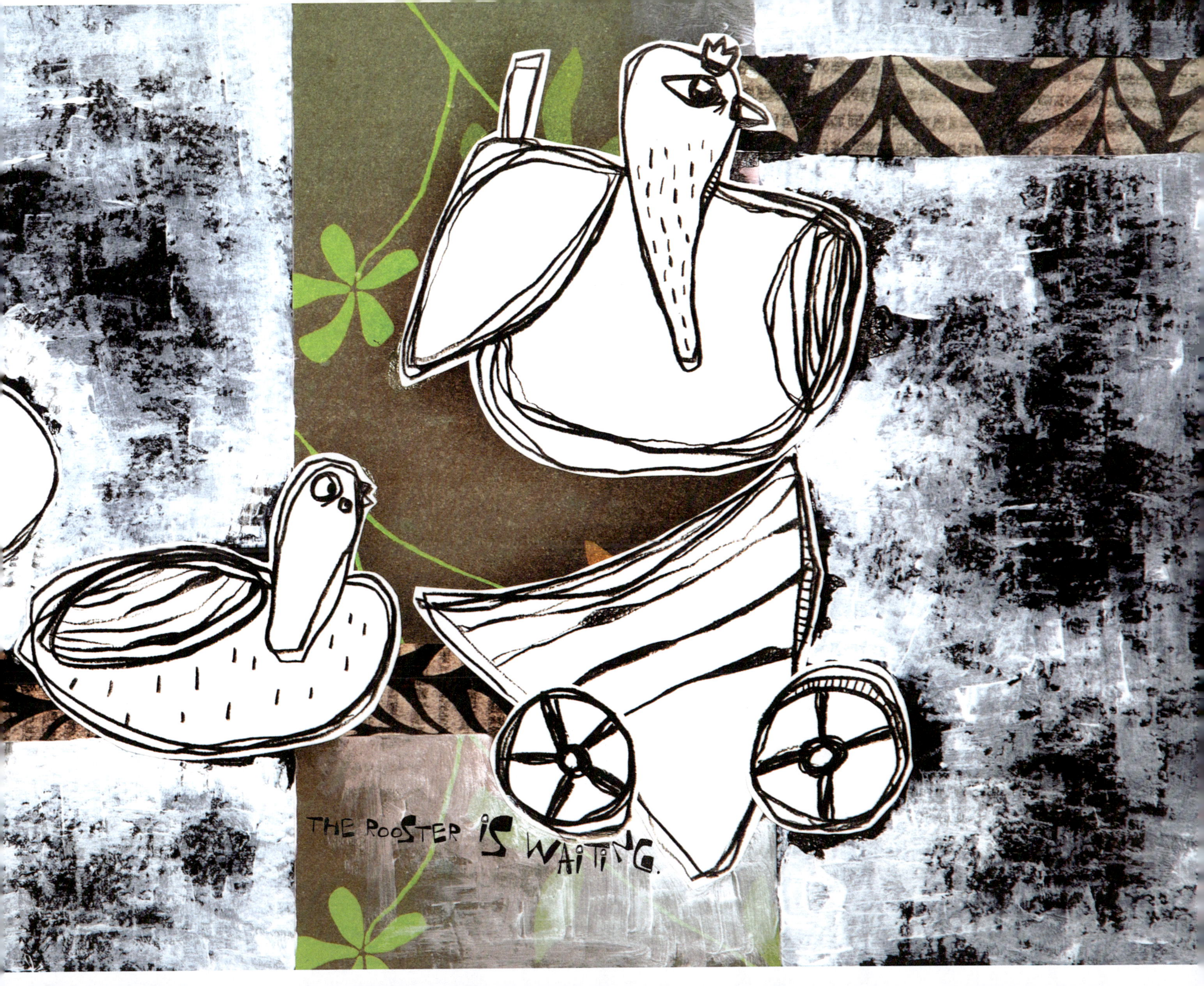
THE ROOSTER IS WAITING.

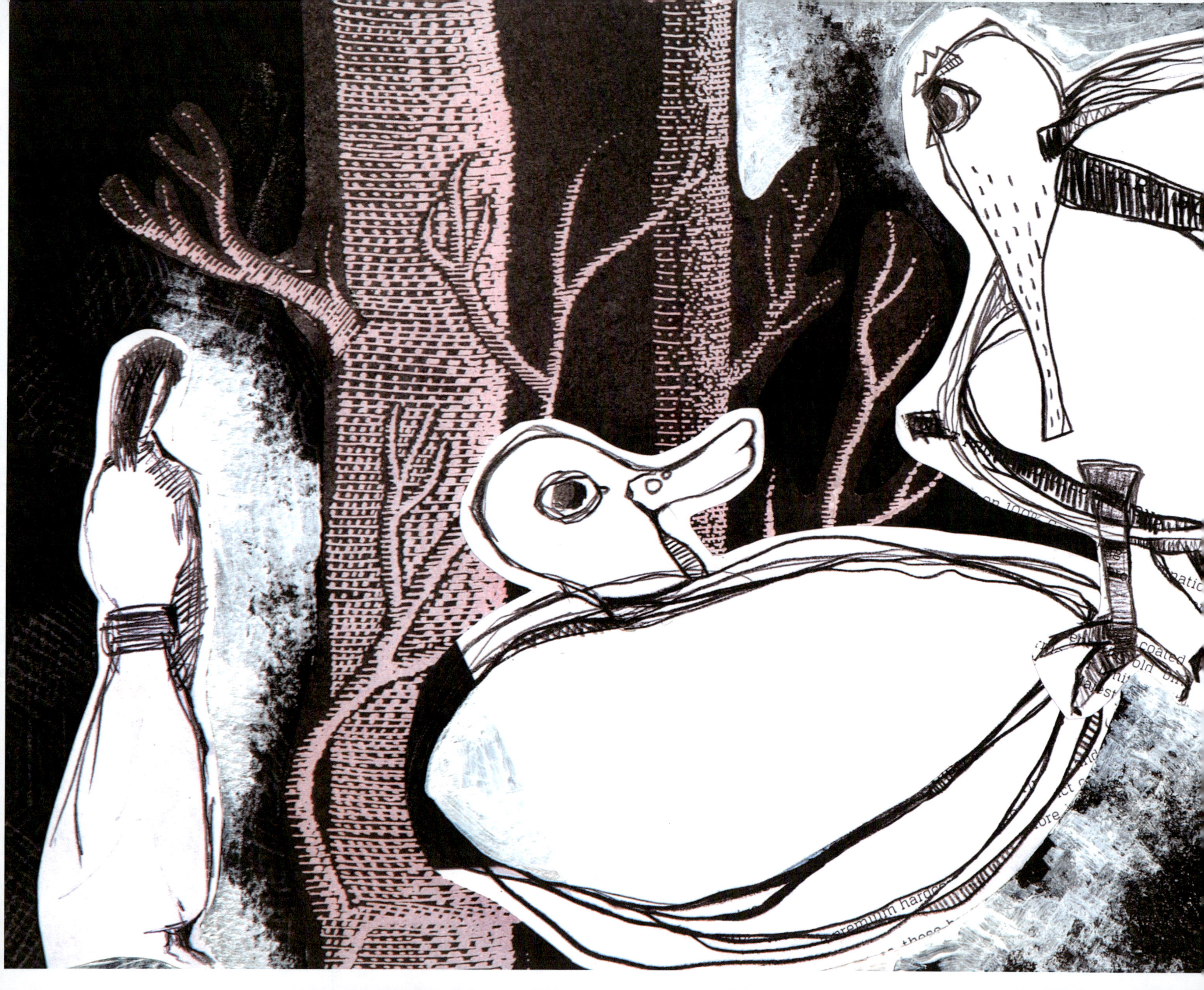

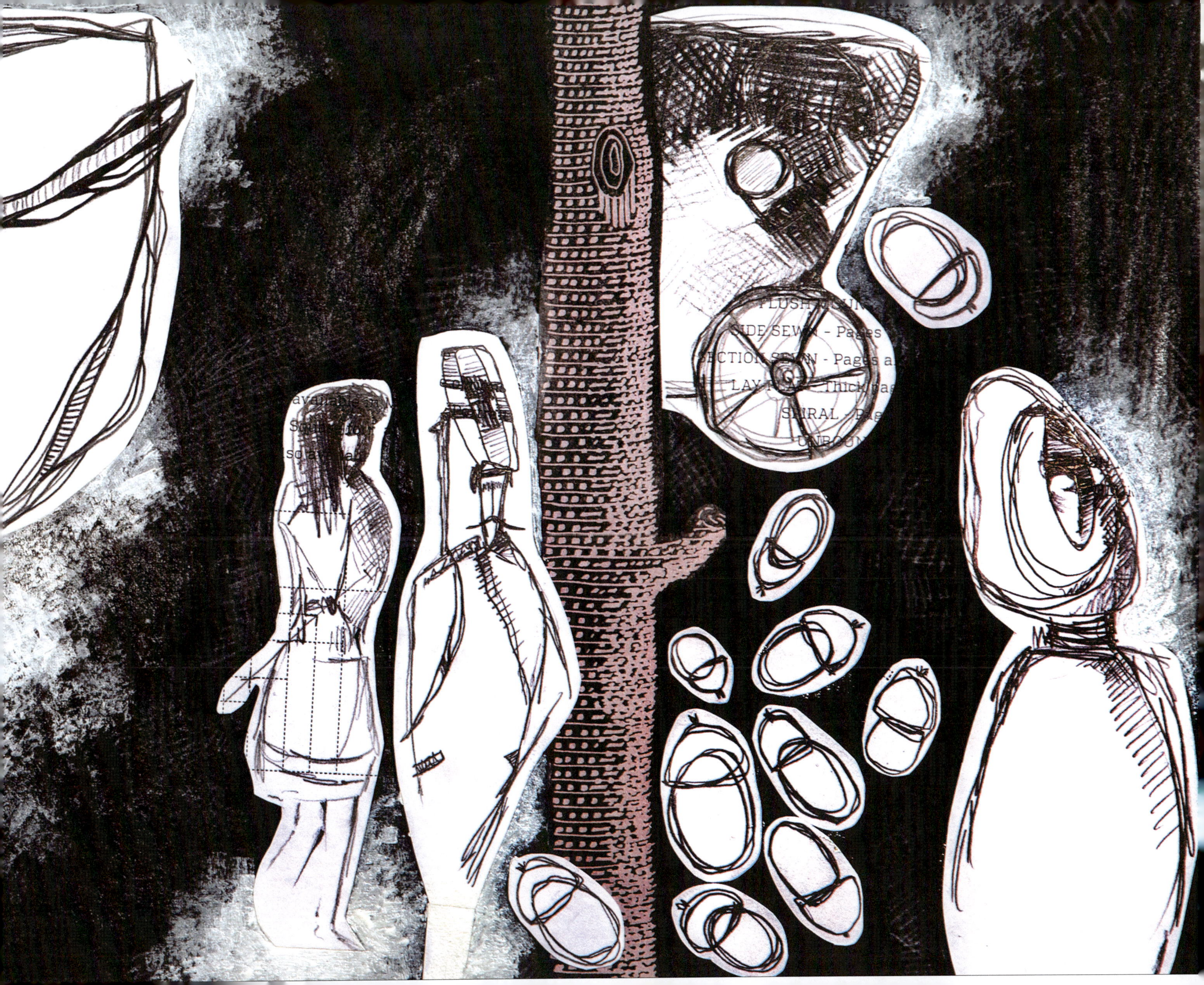
PLUSH BOUND
SIDE SEWN - Pages
SECTION SEWN - Pages a
LAY-FLAT - Thick pa
SPIRAL - Pg
UNBOUND

THE ROOSTER AND THE DUCK ARE FIGHTING.

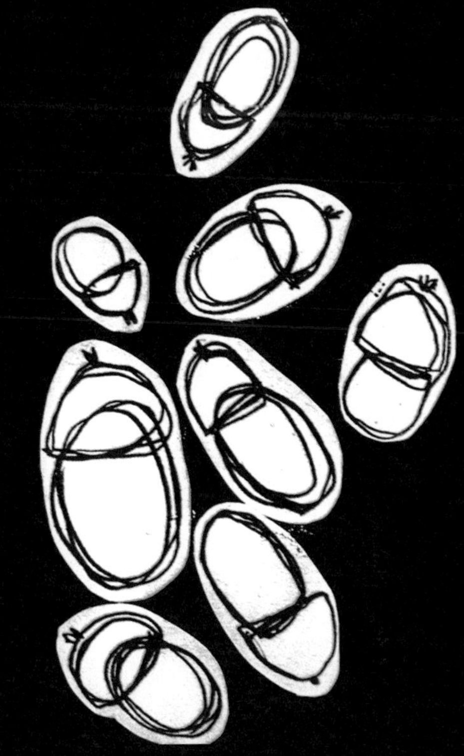

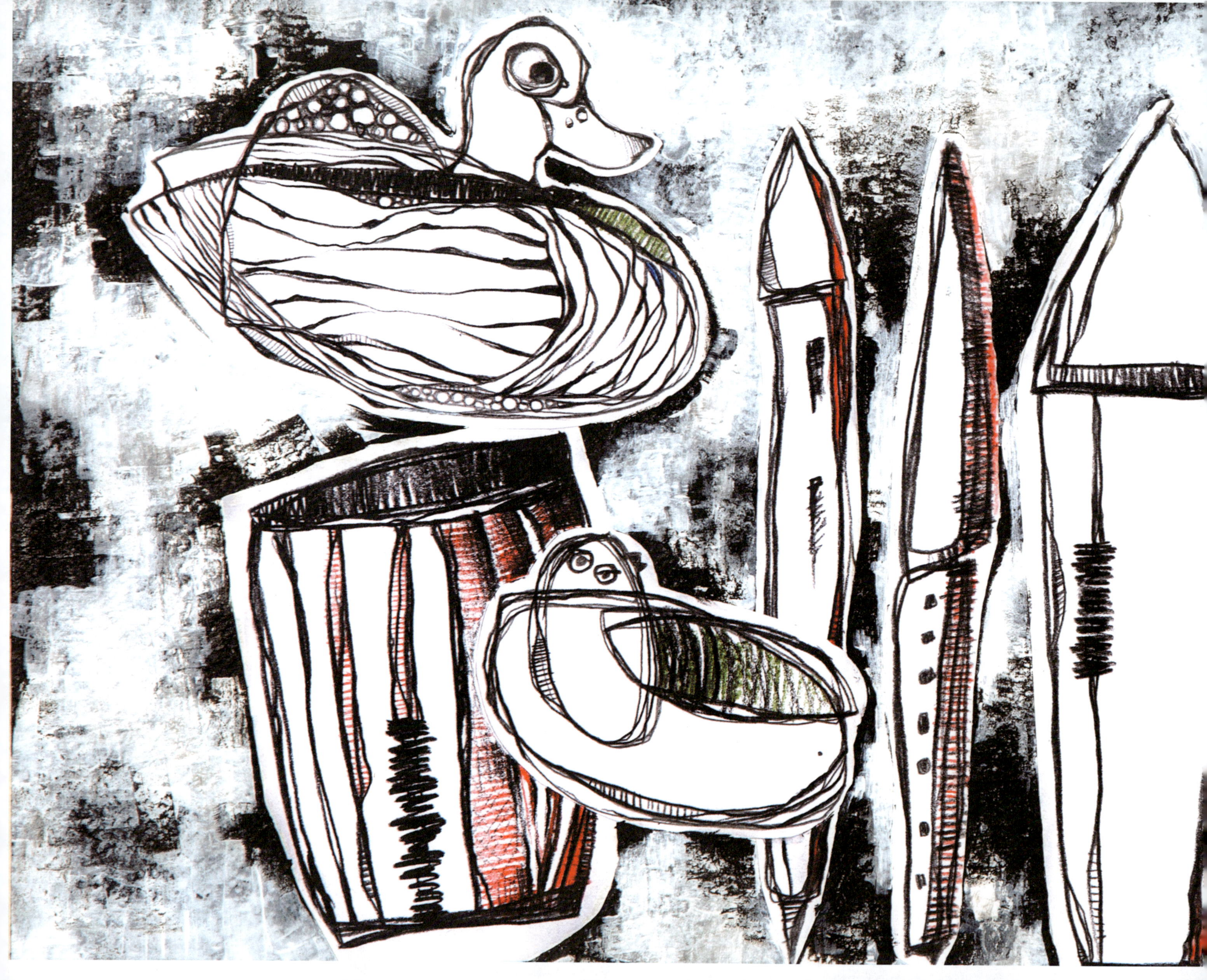

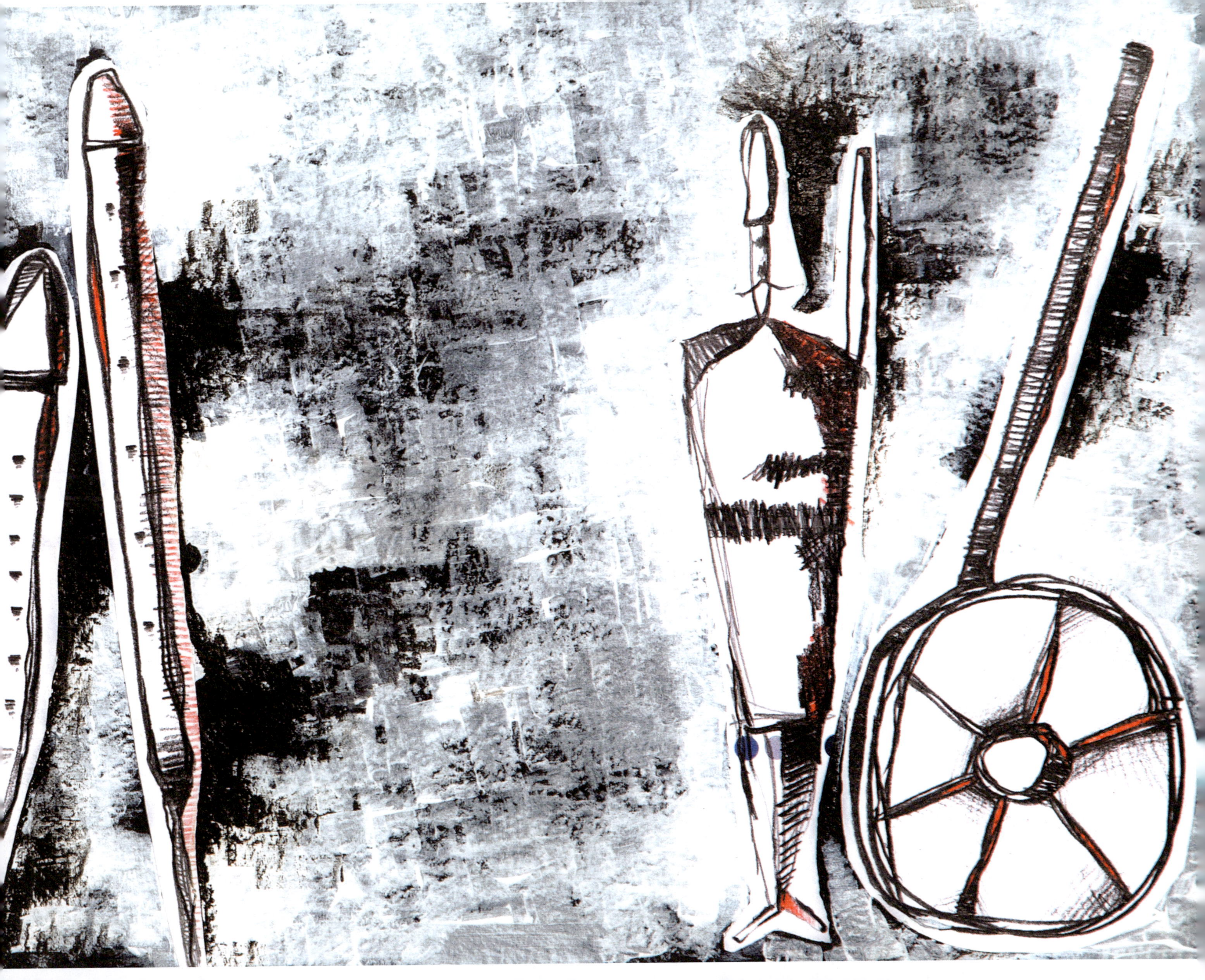

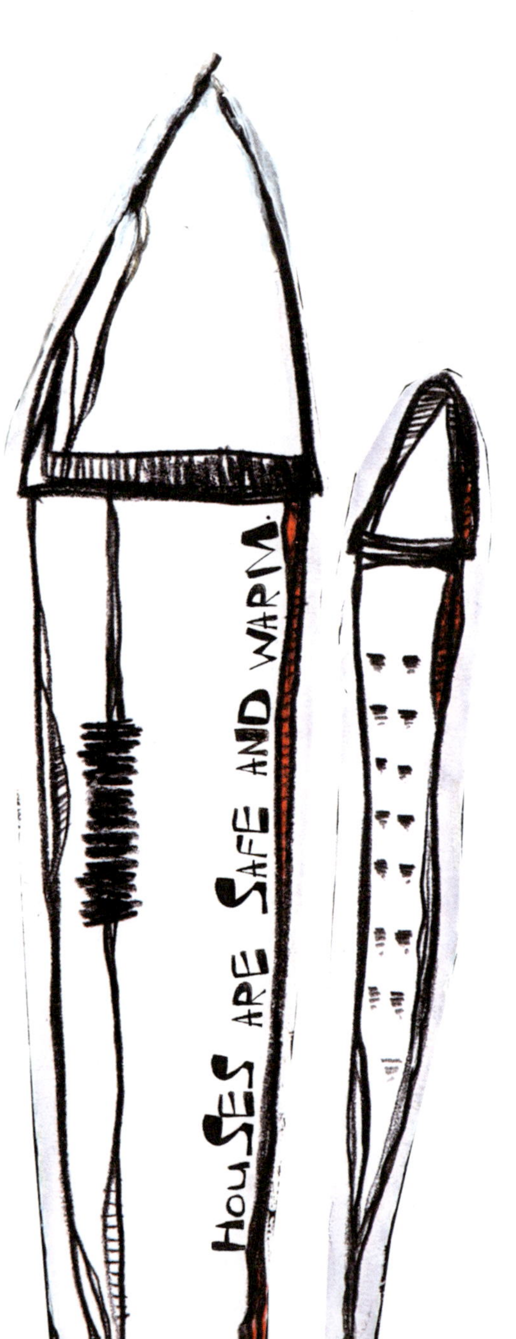

HOUSES ARE SAFE AND WARM.

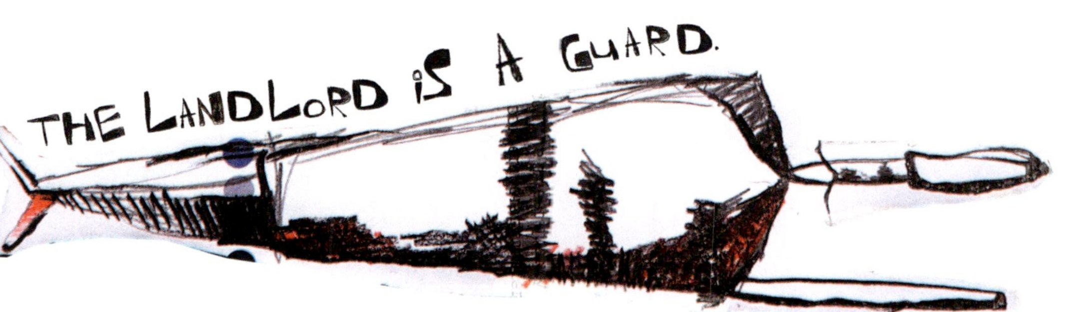

THE LANDLORD IS A GUARD.

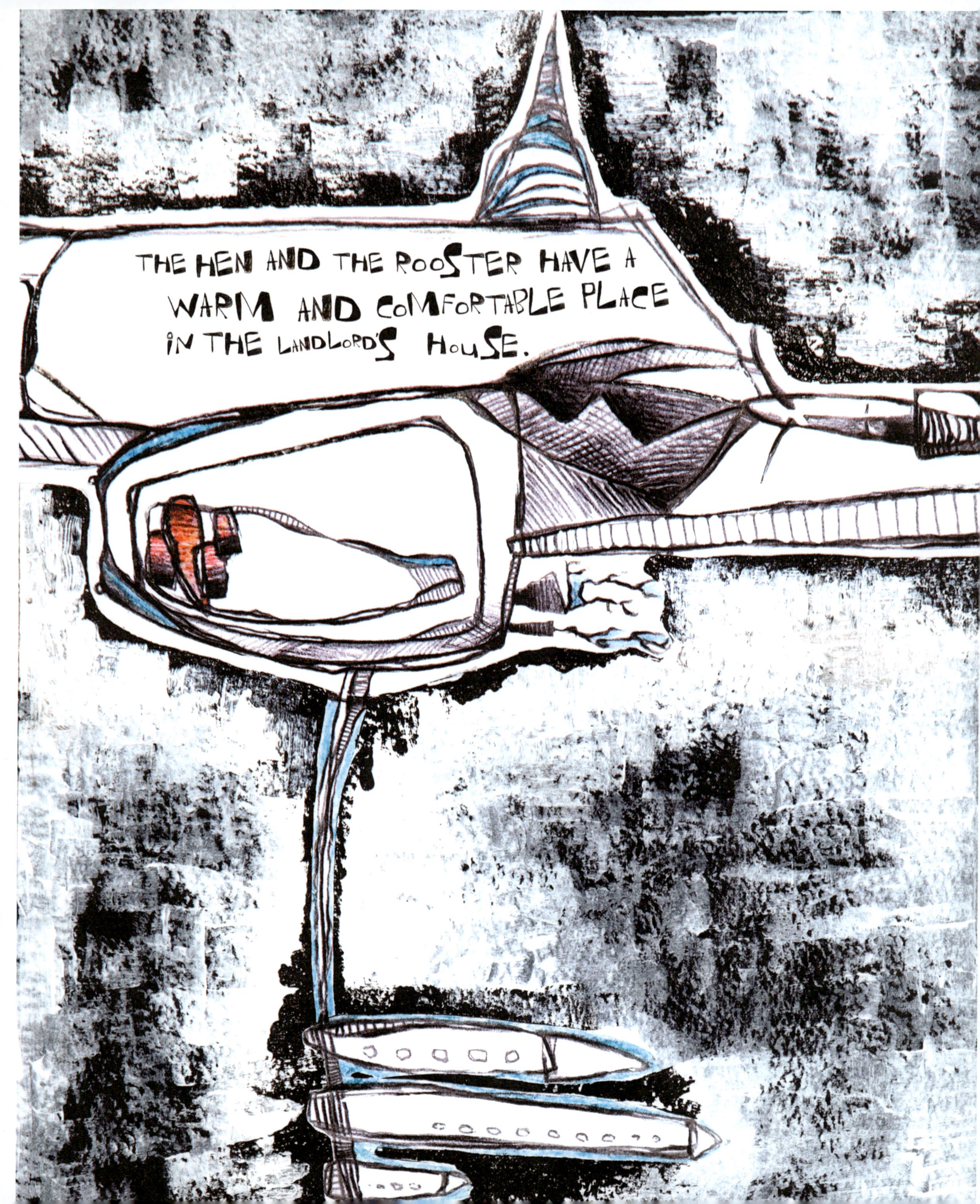

THE HEN AND THE ROOSTER HAVE A WARM AND COMFORTABLE PLACE IN THE LANDLORD'S HOUSE.

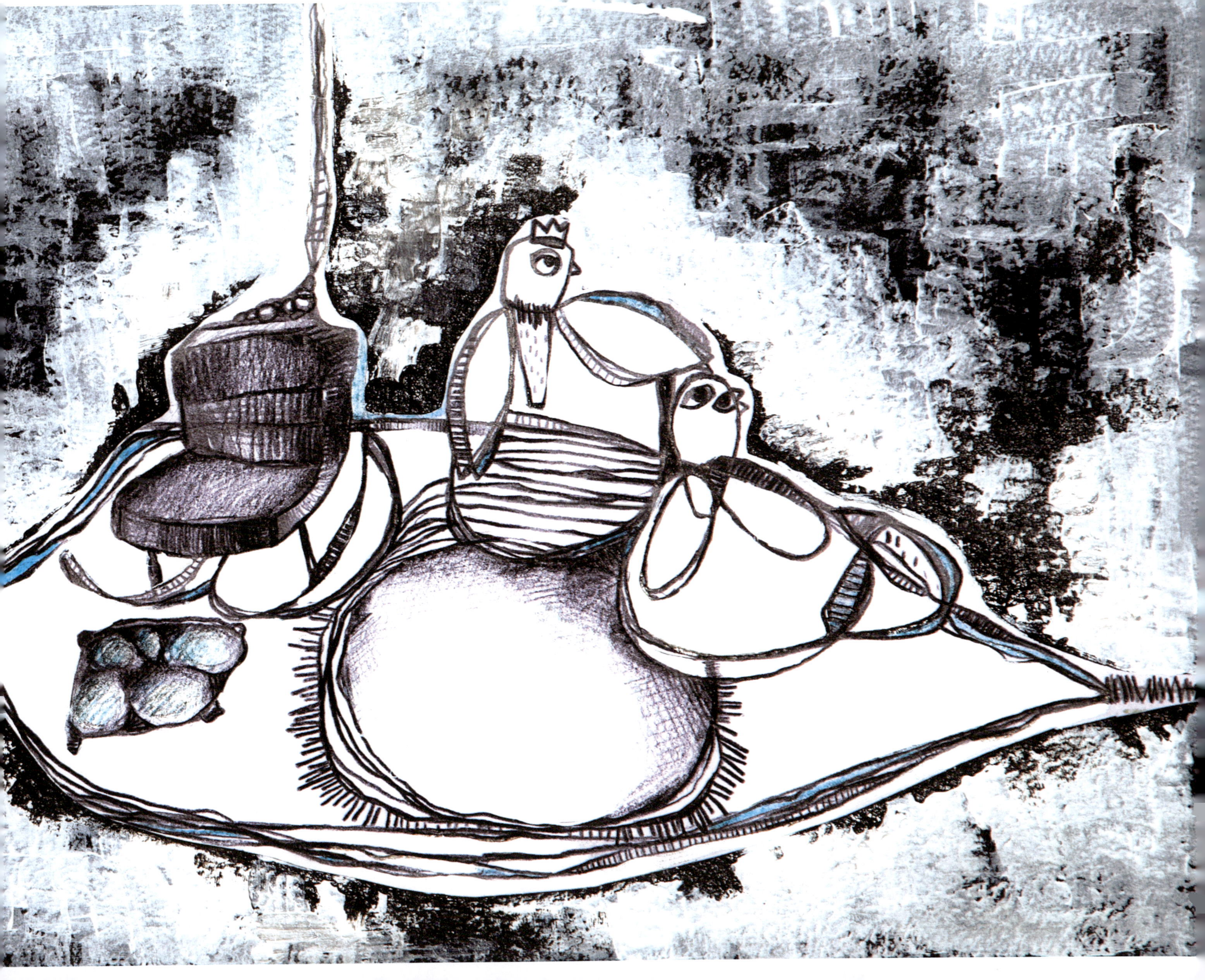

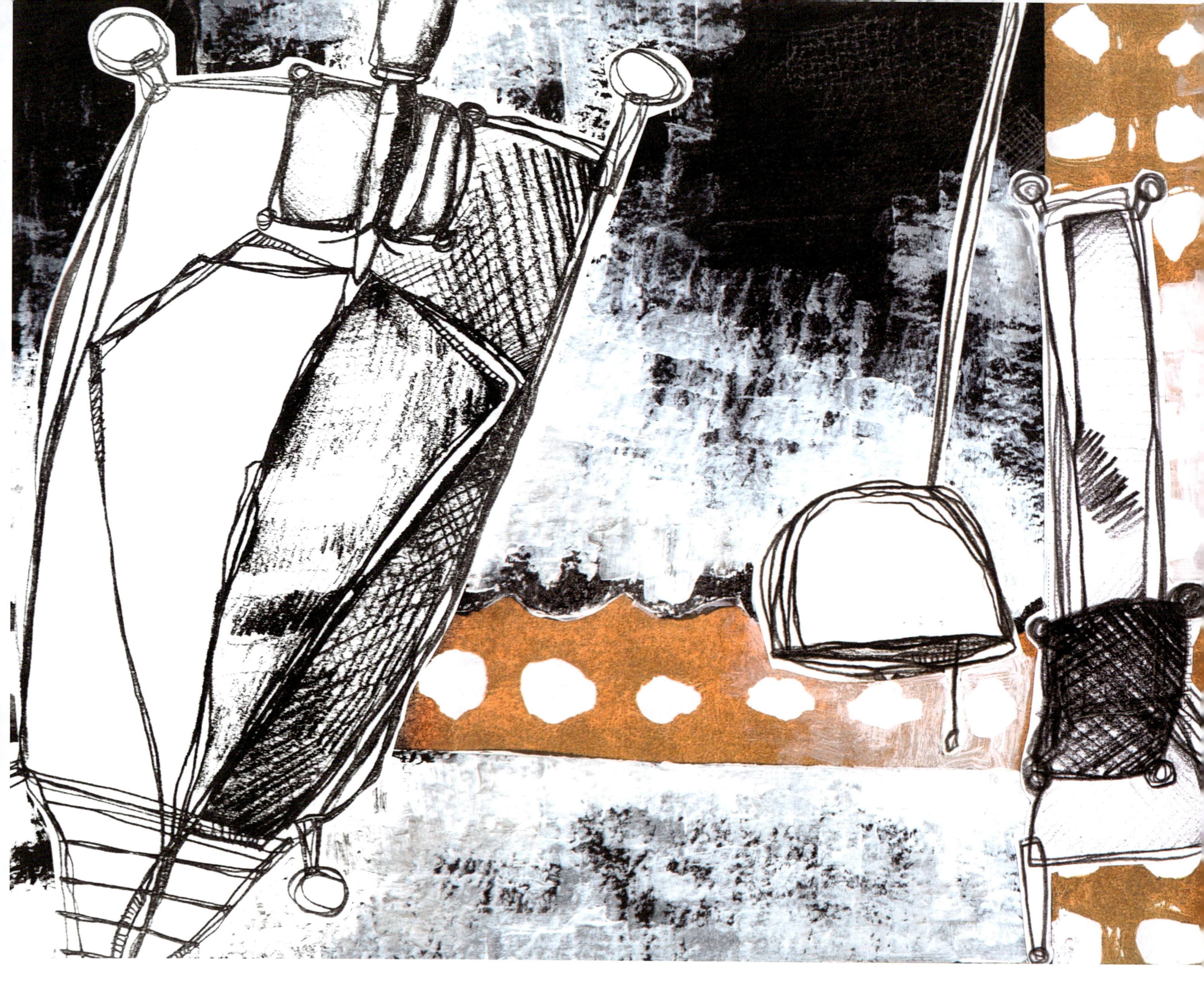

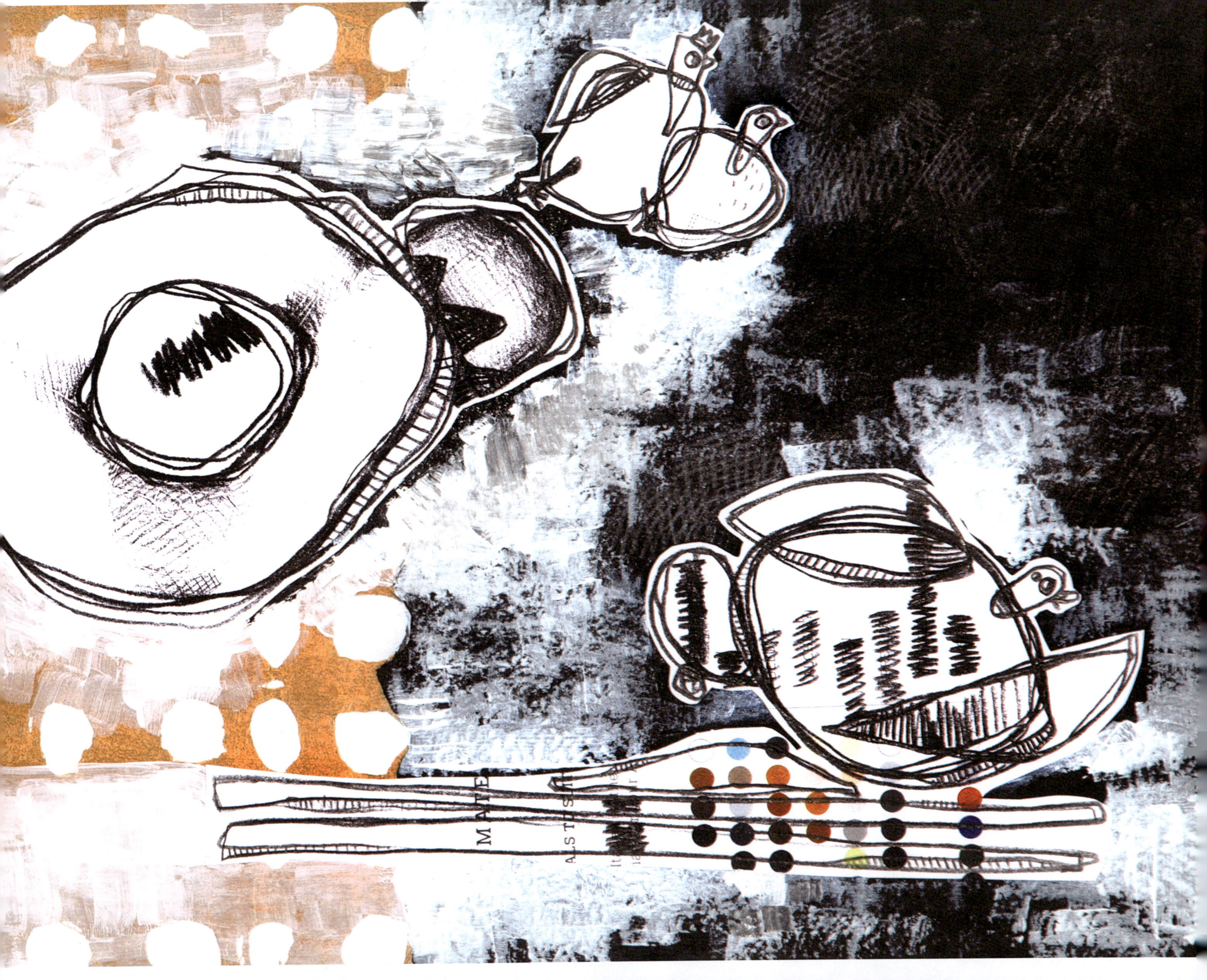

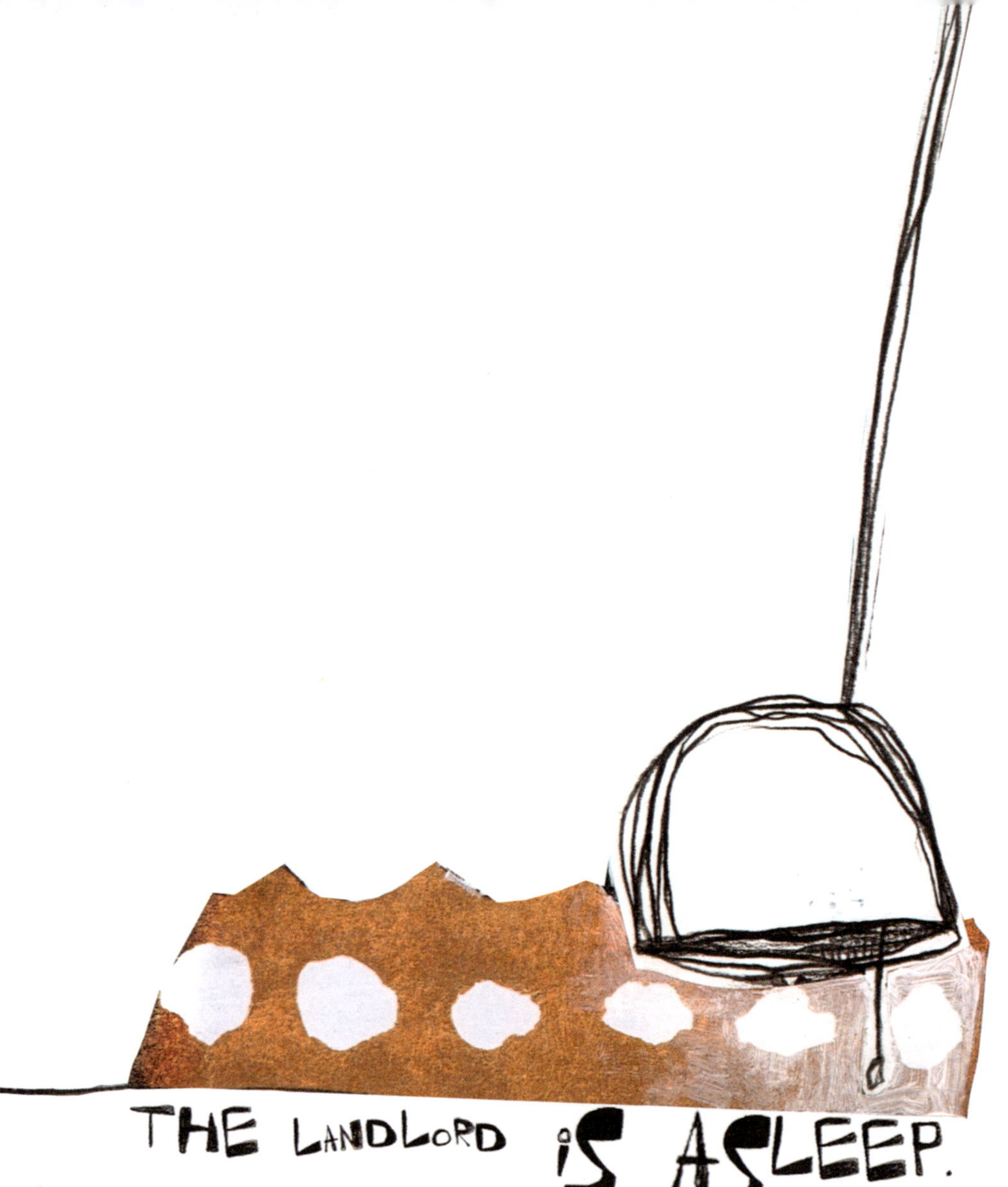
THE LANDLORD IS ASLEEP.

THE HEM AND THE ROOSTER ARE RUNNIG AWAY.

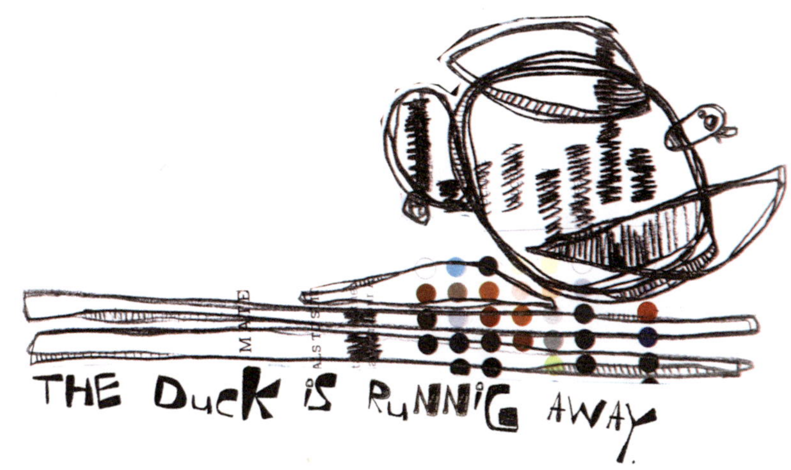

THE DUCK IS RUNNIG AWAY.

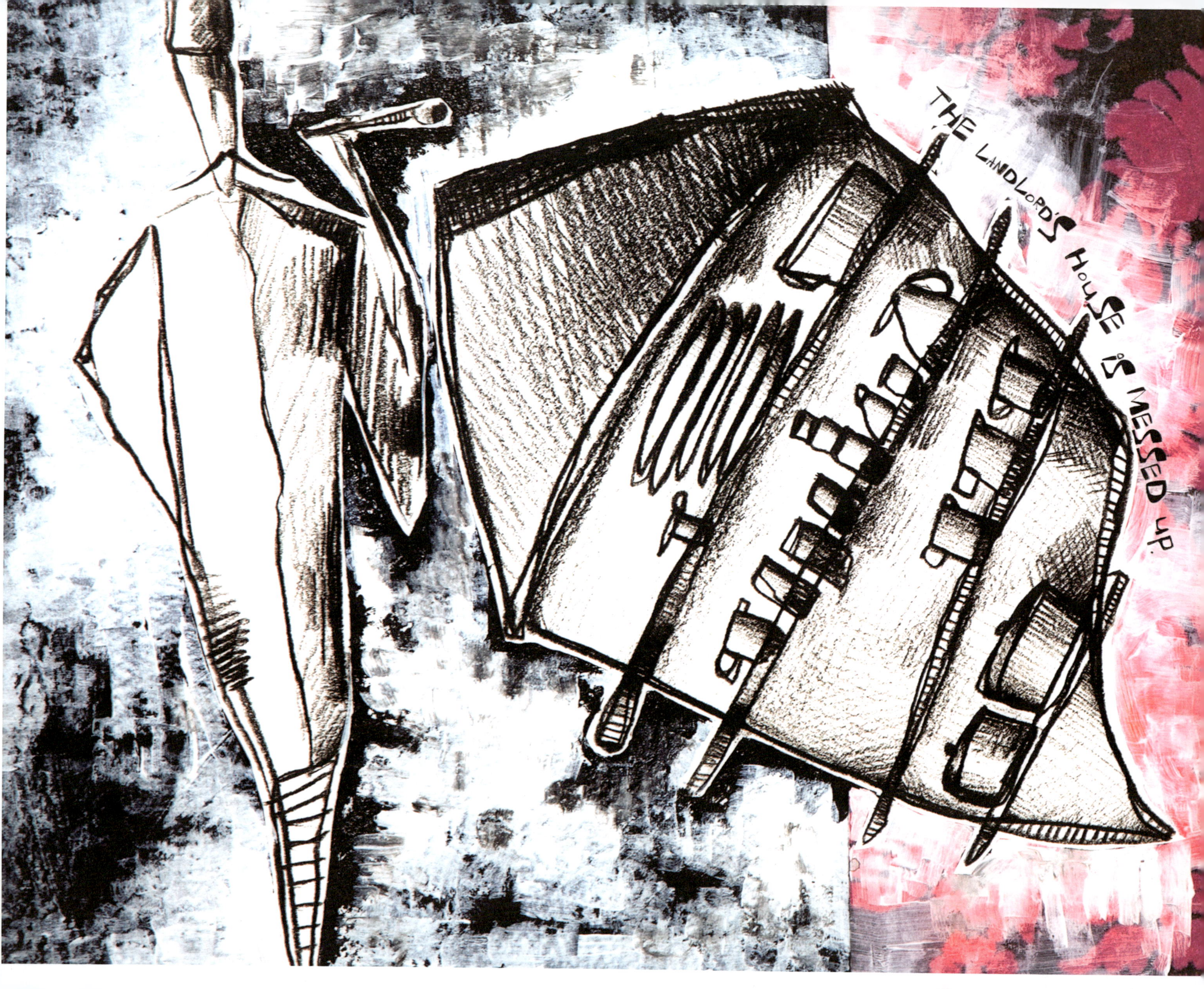

THE LANDLORD'S HOUSE IS MESSED UP.

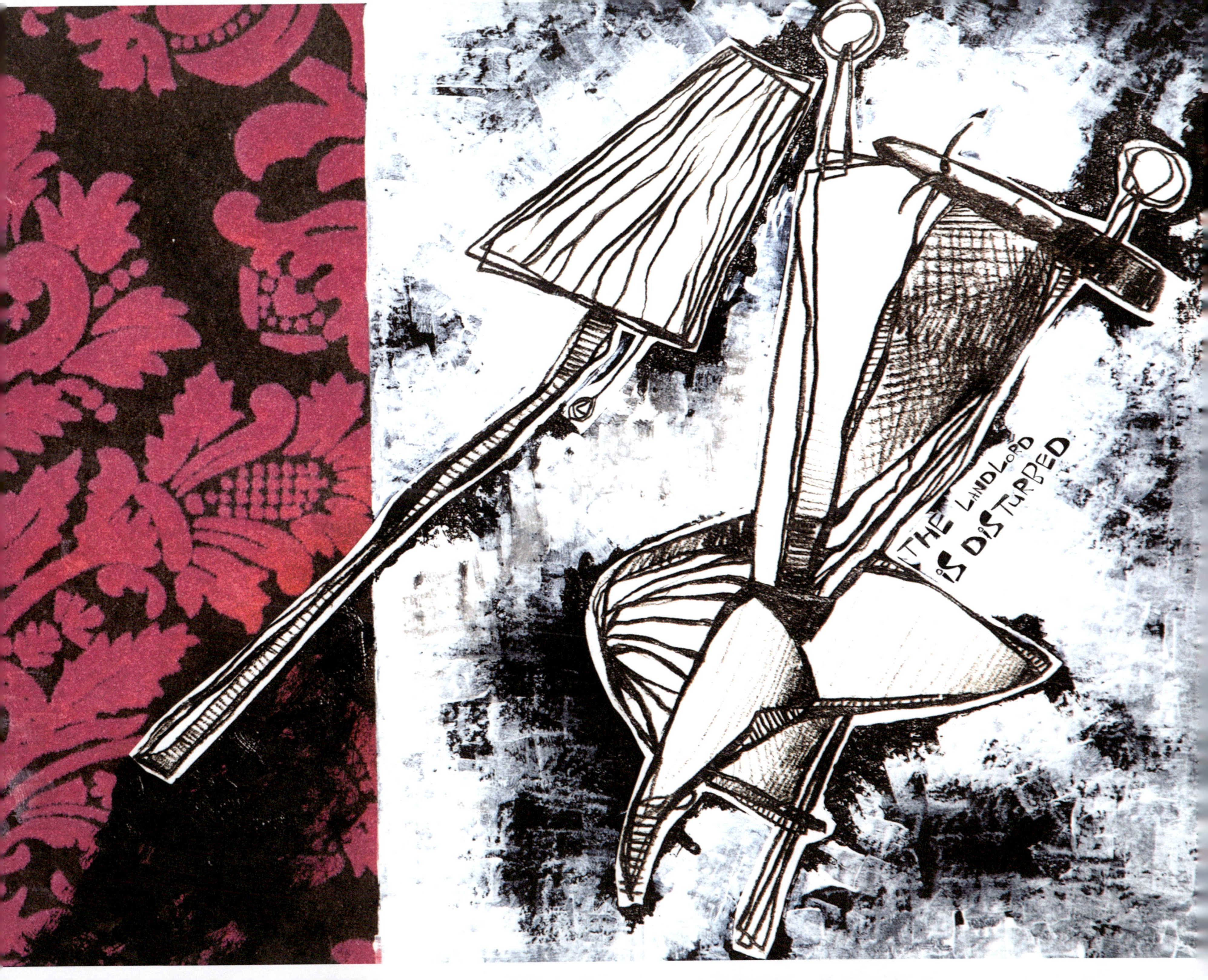

THE LANDLORD
IS DISTURBED.

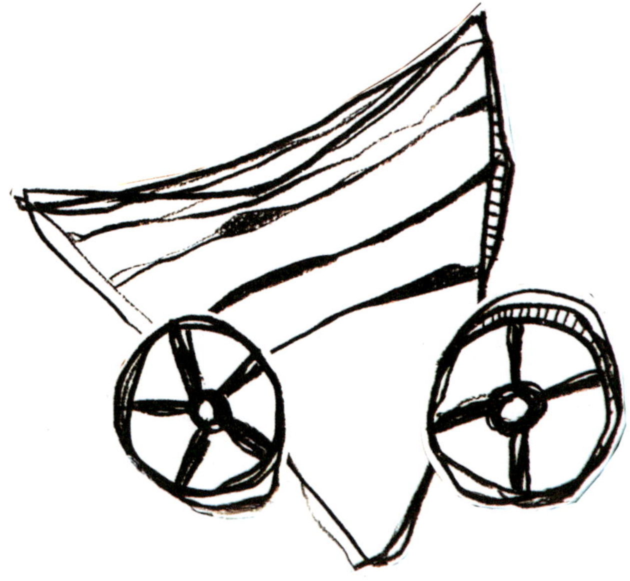

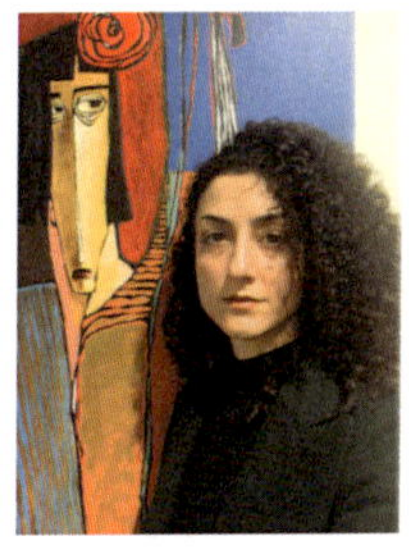

Bahar Taghiani is an illustrator and visual artist. Her love for visual imagery began in her early childhood. She made characters out of pieces of papers and inserted them into an imagery story and gave them life. Her art works are now mostly created using medium such as acrylic, collage, coloured pencil, water colours and they draw inspiration from her perception of the world around her. Bahar is an award winning Unicef illustration competition of " Children on the eve of new year"

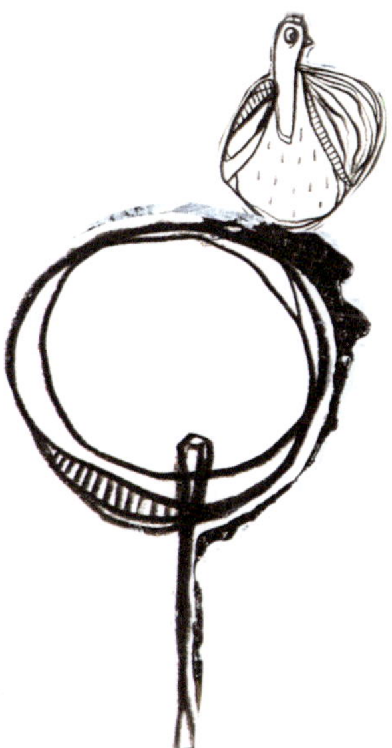

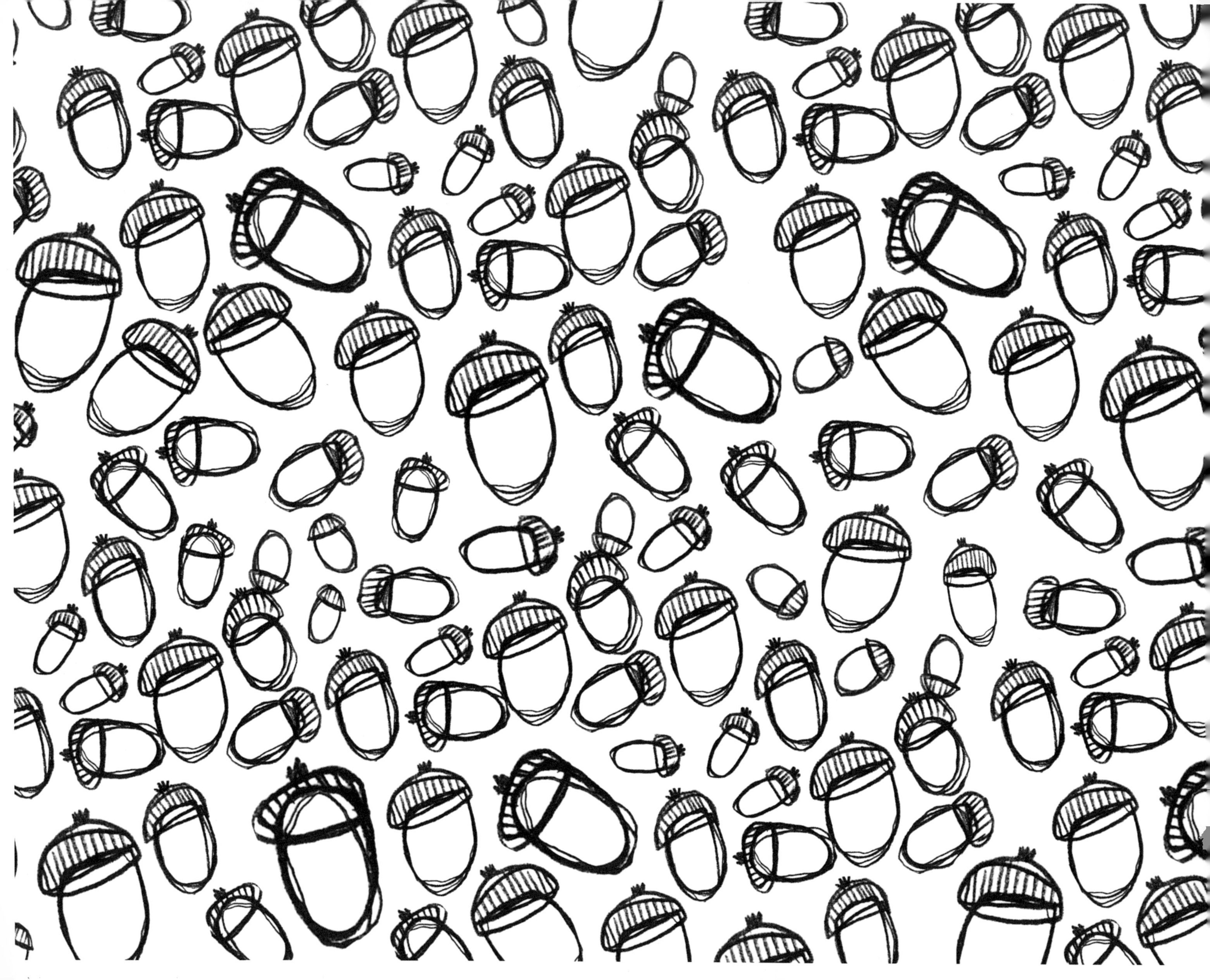

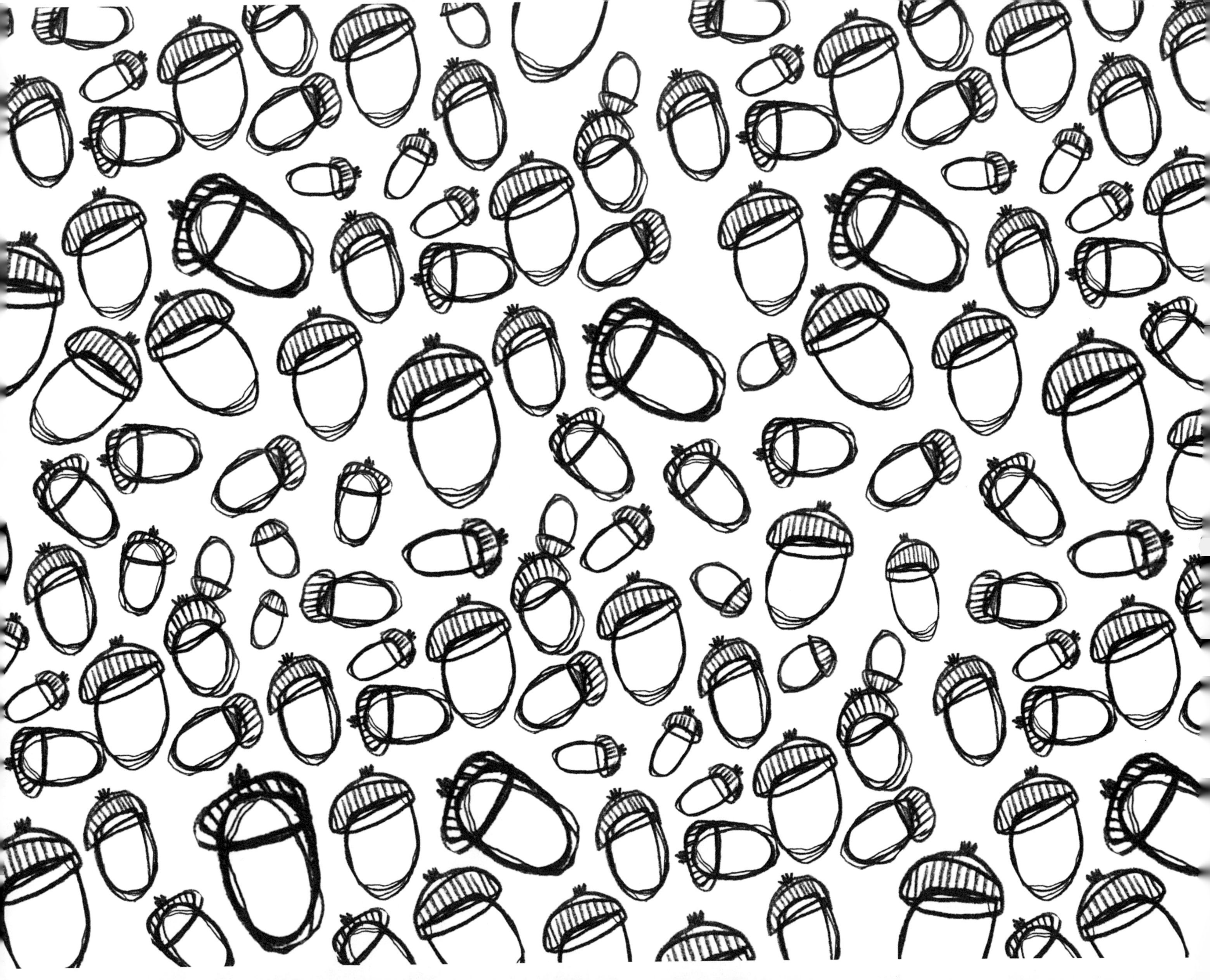

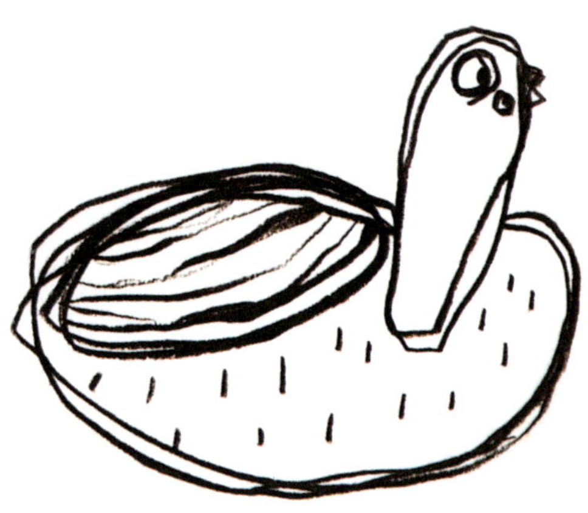

www.ingramcontent.com/pod-product-compliance
Lightning Source LLC
Chambersburg PA
CBRC102239050726
47602CB00014B/171